Gillen.

This booklet was written by Rory Gillen, founder of GillenMarkets, and is also available in eBook format (PDF, ePub or Kindle).

About Gillen

Gillen is a boutique investment advisor offering expert advice on the management of personal, pension and corporate monies. We place a strong emphasis on fully understanding our clients' needs, so that we can make informed decisions and plans, together.

We are investment advisors, not product sellers. Our investment solutions are structured to meet the specific needs of each individual client with minimum assets of €500k.

Our investment advisory fee structure aligns our interests with yours, ensuring that we sit on the same side of the table as our clients.

With our fee structure, there are:

- No upfront commissions or fees payable by clients.

- No dealing costs.

- No early redemption penalties.

- No VAT.

Just a transparent 1.0% annual advisory fee on the assets under advice.

We also offer a subscription-based investment newsletter for do-it-yourself investors and training courses both in-person and online for those wishing to learn more about the principles of sound investing.

We believe trust is earned. Our belief is that we work for clients, looking at each individual's needs and taking a commonsense, long term approach.

We have built an outstanding team with the depth of knowledge and experience to meet all our clients' investment needs. We have an appetite for learning and sharing and we always partner with our clients as equals.

We'd like to hear from you!

Contact details

T: + 353 (0)1 287 1400
E: info@gillenmarkets.com
W: www.gillenmarkets.com

Follow us on Facebook, LinkedIn, Twitter and Gillenmarkets.com.

ILTB Ltd (trading as Gillen/GillenMarkets) is regulated by the Central Bank of Ireland.

Intelligent Gold Investing

Including a section on Bitcoin

(2nd edition / 2023)

A **GillenMarkets** Publication

Rory Gillen

Published by Oak Tree Press, Cork T12 XY2N
www.oaktreepress.com / www.SuccessStore.com

© 2023 ILTB Ltd t/a GillenMarkets

A catalogue record of this book is available from the British Library.

ISBN 978 1 78119 571 0 (Paperback)
ISBN 978 1 78119 572 7 (PDF)
ISBN 978 1 78119 573 4 (ePub)
ISBN 978 1 78119 574 1 (Kindle)

Disclaimer
Investing carries risk and none of the stocks or funds highlighted in this booklet
constitute a recommendation by the author, GillenMarkets or the publisher and
none of these parties can assume liability for any losses that may be sustained
should a reader subsequently invest in them, and any such liability is hereby
disclaimed. Readers should take professional advice before making any investment.
None of the material in this publication constitutes investment advice or an offer to
invest in any of the funds referred to. No one receiving this publication should treat it as a
personal recommendation as it does not take into account the needs and objectives,
personal circumstances, including investment experience, financial position, or attitude to
risk of recipients.

Warning
Past performance is not a reliable guide to future performance.

CONTENTS

Gillen.

Other Publications from GillenMarkets

3 STEPS TO INVESTMENT SUCCESS (2012)

How to Obtain the Returns While Controlling the Risk

Rory Gillen

A PATH TO FINANCIAL FREEDOM (2nd edition / 2023)

A Guide to Sound Investing

Rory Gillen

TIMING THE MARKETS (2023)

Unemotional Approaches to Making Buy & Sell Decisions in Markets

Rory Gillen

BRICKS & MORTAR THROUGH STOCKS & SHARES (2023)

Property Investing in the Stock Markets

Darren Gillen

PRIVATE EQUITY: ACCESS FOR ALL (2023)

Investing in Private Equity through the Stock Markets

Jonathan Yates

UNDERSTANDING ALTERNATIVE ASSETS (2nd edition / 2023)

Gold, Forestry, Government & Corporate Bonds, Renewable Energy & Hedge Strategies

Rory Gillen

All available in print and ebook formats from
GillenMarkets.com, SuccessStore.com & Amazon

INTRODUCTION

Gold is money and has been accepted as such for over 5,000 years. Money serves two purposes: as a medium of exchange in trade and as a store of wealth. As gold generates no income, it is difficult to value in a conventional sense.

Gold has been an excellent store of wealth over the millennia, principally reflecting the limited supplies and its unique physical characteristics, particularly the fact that it does not degrade with time. Gold, however, has never been an ideal medium of exchange in trade largely because the annual new supplies of gold, at *circa* 2%, have not been sufficient to facilitate the expansion in global trade.

Gold is an effective inflation hedge and a proven store of value against all currencies over long-term horizons. But, at times, the gold price can become significantly overvalued against long-term inflationary trends, so that it is not an effective short-term or even medium-term inflation hedge.

Good quality companies and property assets, too, have protected investors against the ravages of inflation, even if in many cases only with a lag. But these assets are no protection in war-torn regions of the world controlled by dictators, despots and totalitarian regimes. There was only one asset that protected German savers over the 1916 to 1945 period that encompassed the two World Wars: gold. Bank deposits and government bonds were all wiped out by hyperinflation, while property and businesses often didn't survive the physical destruction wrought by war, as well as the confiscation of assets by the regime.

As gold covers some critical risks for investors, it represents, in our view, one of the five major asset classes which also include equities, bank deposits, fixed income government bonds and inflation-linked government bonds.

In this booklet, we take a look at the history of gold, its unique physical characteristics, when the price of gold has matched or beaten inflation and when it has lagged. In terms of attempting to determine an intrinsic value for gold, we compare the current gold price to the US consumer price index over time, against the US average house price since gold traded freely in the late 1960s and against its own cost of production which has been rising over time, reflecting the rising costs of extraction.

Recognising that determining an intrinsic value for gold is an imprecise science, we put forward three technical indicators that provide a risk-controlled way of determining when gold is likely in an uptrend and worth owning. All three indicators have outperformed a 'Buy & Hold' gold strategy since 1968 by healthy margins. Two of those three indicators are currently in 'Buy' mode.

Lastly, we highlight how an investor can gain exposure to the ancient metal of the kings.

Enjoy the read.

Rory Gillen
March 2023

1: THE HISTORY OF GOLD

Gold is a fascinating metal and is more than a mere commodity; it is the oldest currency in the world and can rightfully claim its place as the only currency to have acted as a true store of value over the millennia.

Chart 1: Gold Price per Troy Ounce

Source: World Gold Council & GillenMarkets

One only has to be reminded of the fate of the German Reichsmark after World Wars I and II and, more recently, the Zimbabwe dollar, the Russian ruble, the Argentinian peso, the Turkish lira, and the Syrian pound to name but a few, following wars, inflation and government mismanagement of a nation's finances, to understand the value of owning an international currency that cannot be printed (debased) at will.

On their own and without the aid of the European Central Bank, the Irish, Portuguese and Greek currencies would probably have collapsed during or shortly after the Global Financial Crisis (GFC). Equally, local property assets and local businesses that earn substantially all of their money in the local economy do not protect investors from government ineptitude or profligacy.

In contrast, gold is an international currency and is unaffected by what governments are up to in local economies. International property and business assets also provide protection for investors against the vagaries of their own local economy and currency.

Gold competes for investor attention along with the other major asset classes – equities, physical property, government and corporate bonds, inflation-linked bonds and bank deposits. Gold generates no income so that its primary role in an investment portfolio is as a store of value, as it protects against inflation, breakdowns in paper-based banking systems and/or wars.

In terms of risk protection, gold is a real asset and not someone else's liability. In comparison, all paper currencies are IOUs from banks (but ultimately central banks and governments) and, in that regard, each paper currency reflects money a bank owes you, the depositor. As savers saw during the GFC, banks aren't always in a position to honour their bank deposits. In other words, owning paper money or saving *via* bank deposits comes with counter-party risk. Not so with gold or any of the precious metals!

In addition, of course, there is nothing to stop banks and central banks printing unlimited quantities of new monies and degrading the value of existing monies in circulation. In comparison, new gold cannot be mined at will. According to the World Gold Council, there is *circa* 210,000 metric tonnes of gold above ground. Mining production annually is running at *circa* 3,600 tonnes, which is adding less than 2% to the existing gold supplies annually.

The global market in gold is small compared to paper currencies. At the current price of $1,836 an ounce (24th February 2023), 210,000 tonnes are worth *circa* $12.5 trillion. That's just 40% of US Government debt outstanding and just 4% of global government debt outstanding. While gold is money and has been the best store of value over the millennia, there just isn't enough gold around for it to act as medium of exchange in trade.

Finance for trade, or credit, needs to be able to expand at the same rate as economic activity and for this reason credit, or paper money, long ago replaced gold as the facilitator of trade. The difficulty for paper money, or credit, is that the amount in circulation can also be expanded at a faster rate than is justified by the natural growth in trade or general economic activity, leading to inflation.

In that regard, gold acts as a far better store of value given that new supplies of gold cannot be introduced at will.

The Physical Attributes of Gold

No discussion on gold, of course, would be complete without an understanding of its unique physical attributes, which have made it both a desirable possession (jewellery) and a suitable protector of wealth over the millennia.

Gold is the heaviest metal; it has the highest density. It is virtually indestructible, impossible to create artificially and difficult to counterfeit. Its melting point is 1,064 degrees Celsius. It is the most stretchable pure metal known to man – a single gram can be crafted into a sheet one metre squared, which is so thin that the sun can shine through. It does not oxidise (rust) in air or water; it has no taste in its purest form; it is chemically unreactive and non-toxic to the human body, and it is an excellent conductor of electricity.

Its physical beauty has seen it used as jewellery for thousands of years and, more recently, its robustness and dependability has seen it in increasing demand in many new complex industrial applications, where price is less of a consideration.

In geological terms, gold-bearing rock is rare and, even when it is discovered, an average tonne of gold ore currently yields less than three to four grams of gold – that is three to four parts to a million – and even this figure has been declining over time, although ongoing advances in drilling technology continue to make lower grade deposits economic.

Its durability, rarity and divisibility make it valuable and tradable, and allow significant wealth to be stored or transported with relative ease. It is, therefore, easy to understand how gold has been an accepted form of money for thousands of years. Unlike commodities in general, gold can be stored and transported easily and at low cost, which means that it can be bought and held as an investment without fear that costs will overly impact returns, and it does not perish with time.

2: IS GOLD AN INFLATION HEDGE?

There is an old saying that goes *"an ounce of gold in the early 1900s bought you a good quality suit in New York, and it still does"* – in other words, gold has maintained its purchasing power over not just decades, but over centuries. One cannot say the same for paper currencies; throughout history all paper currencies have eventually lost all of their purchasing power (value).

The simple answer to the question in the chapter title is "Yes. Gold is an inflation hedge over the long-term". But it is not necessarily an inflation hedge in the short- or even medium-term. In **Chart 2,** the orange line represents the gold price since 1935, while the dotted green line represents what the price of gold would have been had it simply increased in line with US consumer price inflation (CPI).

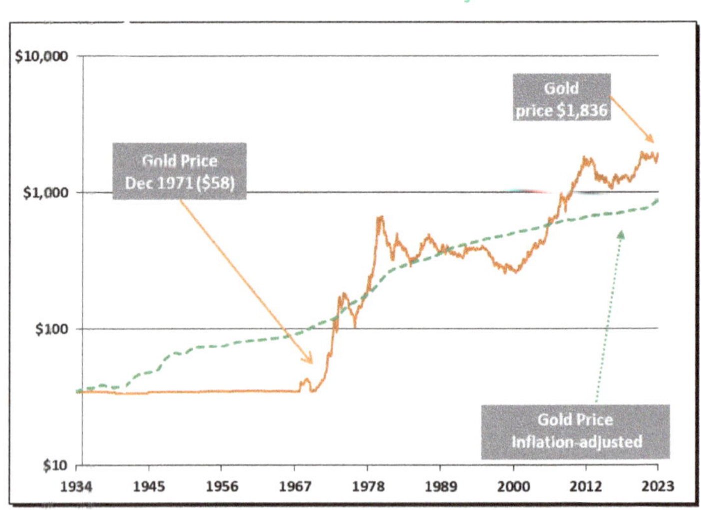

Chart 2: The Gold Price *vs* Inflation-adjusted Gold Price

Source: World Gold Council & GillenMarkets.

The chart starts in 1935 as, at that time, gold was probably fairly priced against the US dollar. In the early to mid-1930s, the incoming President Roosevelt devalued the dollar against gold, in effect acknowledging that the US Government had to increase money and credit in the US economy to overcome the depression and deflationary forces at that time.

The US Government of the time embraced money printing as a way out of its debt constraint and could no longer offer convertibility from dollars to gold at the old rate of $21 a troy ounce that pertained prior to 1933. The gold price was revalued upwards to $35 against the dollar at that time. Said another way, the number of dollars that was now needed to buy an ounce of gold was increased from 21 to 35, a 67% increase. The amount of gold in existence was largely unchanged over this period, so that the supply of dollars in circulation increased by 67%.

Chart 2 highlights that, over the period from 1935 to 2023,[1] the gold price has kept pace, and more, with US consumer price inflation (CPI). As **Table 1** highlights, the gold price has increased at a rate of 4.6% compound *per annum* from 1935 to 2022, while US CPI has increased at a rate of 3.5% compound *per annum*. Over the long-term, then, gold has indeed acted as an inflation hedge.

Table 1: Gold Price Gains compound *per annum*

Period	Gold	US CPI
1935-1969	0.0%	2.9%
1970s	30.7%	7.1%
1980s	-2.4%	5.5%
1990s	-3.3%	3.0%
2000s	14.3%	2.4%
2010s	3.3%	2.0%
2020s	6.2%	1.8%
1935 - 2022	4.6%	3.5%

Source: US Bureau of Economic Analysis / GillenMarkets.

But, as **Table 1** also highlights, gold has not been a consistent inflation hedge over shorter-term time intervals.

---

[1] Closing price of gold on 24th February 2023.

From late 1934 until 1969, the dollar was pegged to the gold price at an exchange rate of $35 an ounce of gold. This was despite heavy spending by the US government during the 1940s (World War II) and the 1960s (Vietnam War), and the consequent rise in US Government debt levels. In August 1971, the newly-elected President Nixon ended the Federal Reserve's commitment to exchange dollars for gold at a rate of $35 an ounce.

Quite simply, the increase in US dollars in circulation and rising inflation by the late 1960s led to investor nervousness regarding the dollar as a store of value and overseas central banks started asking for payment from the US in gold rather than dollars. The US's gold supplies would soon have been exhausted. In terms of purchasing power, gold had become too cheap against the US dollar.

As **Table 1** highlights, inflation averaged 2.9% annually from 1935 to 1969, while the price of gold stood still over the same period (because the gold price was regulated over this period and did not trade freely). We can say with certainty that, as the US Government was prepared to supply gold at a fixed exchange rate against dollars from 1935 to 1969, the gold price could not keep pace with inflation, and it did not provide investors with an inflation hedge over that 35-year period.

With the US Federal Reserve no longer willing to supply gold at a fixed rate of one ounce of gold for $35 from mid-1971 onwards, and the demand for gold increasing because of the outbreak of inflation, the gold price shot upwards in the 1970s. Inflation also picked up pace in the early 1970s and increased at 7.1% compound *per annum* during the entirety of the 1970s. The gold price, however, did far better rising by 30.7% compound *per annum*, reflecting the fact that (i) it entered the 1970s undervalued relative to US inflation and (ii) there existed excessive investor demand due to fears of ongoing runaway inflation. Unquestionably, then, gold was a terrific inflation hedge in the 1970s.

However, as **Chart 2** highlights, having entered the 1970s considerably undervalued compared to recorded consumer price inflation (since 1935), gold entered the 1980s considerably overvalued relative to the long-term consumer price inflationary trend.

So, while the 1970s offered gold investors wonderful returns, difficult times lay ahead. The late 1970s ushered in a new US central banker, Paul Volcker, who was determined to end excessive inflation.

Source: Bloomberg.

As **Chart 3** highlights, Volcker raised US interest rates significantly in the early 1980s, putting the US economy into recession and changing consumer mentality at the time. Volcker succeeded in reining back inflation and ushered in a period of declining inflation, or disinflation.

With gold having entered the 1980s overvalued relative to the underlying inflation trend, it did poorly against inflation during both the 1980s and 1990s, recording negative returns when inflation was still positive but under control (see **Table 1**). More specifically, the gold price declined at a rate of 2.4% compound *per annum* in the 1980s and 3.3% compound *per annum* in the 1990s, while inflation averaged *circa* 5.5% through the 1980s and 3.0% through the 1990s.

Like any asset, then, investor over-enthusiasm in the late 1970s lifted the gold price far beyond what could have been justified by the consumer price inflation (CPI) trend. By the early 1980s, then, severe overvaluation compared to recorded inflation left the gold price vulnerable to a period of sub-par returns. The gold bear market lasted from 1980 to 2001. One can say with certainty that gold did not act as an inflation hedge over this 21-year period.

As evidenced in **Chart 2**, the long bear market in gold prices from 1980 to 2001 once again left gold cheap relative to the long-term consumer price inflation trend in the US, and the weakening in the dollar from 2001 along with what investors perceived to be loose monetary policy in response to the 2001-03 recession ignited a new gold bull market. Gold performed well in the 2000s, delivering returns of 14.3% compound *per annum* compared to inflation of 2.4% compound *per annum* over that decade.

But, as **Chart 2** highlights, by the end of the 2000s the gold price was once again well above the underlying consumer price inflationary trend.

The Global Financial Crisis (GFC) in 2008 propelled the gold price further upwards through to 2011, most likely on fears that central bank quantitative easing programmes would ignite inflation. In hindsight, it was a fear-based move in the gold price post the GFC. The inflationary / deflationary arguments that followed the GFC were hotly debated, but deflationary forces won out. Of course, central bank money printing is only one source of (potentially inflationary) money printing or credit creation in an economy. Banks, too, can create money (or credit).

How Banks Create Money or Credit

When a bank grants you a loan, it simply transfers credit, or money, into your account that you can use to spend. That loan, then, becomes a deposit, so that it was the creation of the loan that also created the deposit – *i.e.,* banks don't simply lend out pre-existing deposits, they can actually create new money. Regulations dictate that the bank sets aside some of its own capital to cover the risks of losing money on a loan. Following the GFC, the amount of capital that banks have to hold to cover future possible bad debts has been increased significantly, which has made the banking system more robust.

Clearly, if all depositors demand their deposits back at the same time, the bank will have a liquidity problem. But, typically, so long as depositors have confidence in the solvency of the bank, they tend not to demand their deposits back at the same time. This confidence was eroded coming up to the GFC. Interbank lending seized up (where banks lend to other banks) and bank runs, where depositors demand their money back, started to appear with the first recorded case running up to the Global Financial Crisis being Northern Rock.

But banks can also contract credit and, of course, following the GFC bad loans soared, banks became risk averse and were more interested in getting their loans repaid than making new loans. So, credit or money supply contracted in banking systems in the developed economies following the GFC. While the expansion of money supply created by central banks' quantitative easing programmes helped to provide liquidity in the global economy, to lower the cost of debt and to lift asset prices (to some degree alleviating the bad debt problem) much of that 'newly created money' simply went to improve liquidity in the banks as there was little demand for additional credit from retail or business customers.

As an example of credit contraction, **Table 2** highlights the 'Loans & Other Assets' outstanding at the two main Irish banks in 2007 and 2016.

Table 2: Contraction in Irish Banking Assets: 'Loans & Other Assets'

	2007 €bn	2016 €bn	Change
AIB	168.1	95.6	-43%
Bank of Ireland	183.5	123.1	-33%
Combined	**351.6**	**218.7**	**-38%**

Source: Annual reports.

From 2007 to 2016 'Loans & Other Assets' financed by the two main Irish banks contracted 38%. Some of the contraction reflected the disposal of non-core assets (including UK and US banking assets) as the two Irish banks retreated to their core domestic market, but there's no doubt that core 'Loan Books' also contracted.

While the level of contraction in banking assets was not as severe elsewhere in the Eurozone (and was only a temporary phenomenon in the US), we trust the point is clear. So, the problem was deflation, not Inflation, post the GFC.

One could also argue that the deflationary forces reflected a lack of demand for credit, or loans. Consumers and businesses that took on too much debt – and subsequently saw the value of the asset that the debt financed decline – were extremely reluctant to take on any additional debt and were more inclined to pay down debt, leading to deflationary trends. In reality, they are two sides of the same coin!

Entering the 2010s, however, gold was once again well above the price that could be justified by the inflationary trends and vulnerable to a correction. Once investors realised that the threat was not inflation, but deflation, the gold correction got underway. However, overall, for the 2010s, the gold price advanced by a respectable 3.3% compound *per annum versus* US consumer price inflation of 2.0% compound *per annum* over the same period. It's too early to conclude about the likely outcome for the 2020s but, as **Table 2** highlights, the decade has started positively for the gold price.

To sum up, then, gold is an investment against central bank inflationary tendencies, catastrophe in a country's banking system and/or wars. In that regard, gold has proved itself to be an excellent inflation hedge and protector of capital over the long-term, but it is an unreliable inflation hedge over short- or even medium-term horizons.

For investors who want to protect themselves against the risks of future inflation, unless they can convince themselves that gold is either undervalued against long-term inflationary trends – and *Chart 2* suggests otherwise in that regard – they need to invest in assets that provide a more immediate inflation hedge. Normally, inflation-linked government bonds do a better job of it over shorter-term timelines. That said, inflation-linked government bonds are IOUs from a government and vulnerable in a period of war or government insolvency.

Of course, *Chart 2* is not perfect, and we should point out some potential flaws. First, the end point is dependent on the starting point, and starting in 1935 is subjective on our part. Starting earlier or later would result in a different theoretical inflation-adjusted gold price today. We chose the start of 1935 as the dollar was devalued against gold during the early to mid-1930s, so that there is a higher probability that the gold / dollar exchange rate reflected reality at the start of 1935.

Secondly, some argue that US consumer price inflation is under-reported, and we have some sympathy with that view. And, of course, consumer price inflation does not take into account inflation in asset prices. For that reason, we believe that it makes sense to also look at the gold price relative to US asset prices.

Gold Compared to US House Prices

In **Chart 4,** we highlight the gold price against average US house prices. The year 1970 is a reasonable starting point as gold started to trade freely from the late 1960s onwards.

In our view, US house price trends provide a reasonable comparative valuation measure for gold (so long as there's no restriction in housing supply, like in Dublin at present) as a house retains no income or earnings, and is similar to gold in that regard.

Chart 4: Gold Price / US House Price Index Ratio

Source: World Gold Council & Schiller Case US Housing Index.

In contrast, comparing the gold price to, say, the S&P 500 Index over time makes less sense as the S&P 500 Index base increases year-on-year by the amount of earnings retained (not all earnings are paid out by way of dividends).

Chart 4 highlights that, as of end 2022, the gold price-to-US house price index ratio was sitting at 6.4 compared to an average of 5.7 since 1970. On this relative valuation metric, we conclude that gold is currently trading at slightly above fair value relative to the average US house price.

The gold price-to-US house price index ratio has been a sound measure of under and overvaluation of the gold price relative to the average US house price since 1970. Back in the early 1970s, this valuation metric suggested that the gold price was deeply undervalued relative to US house prices. And that preceded a strong rise in the gold price over the subsequent decade. The same relative valuation metric suggested that the gold price was similarly undervalued compared to US house prices by the early 2000s and gold then enjoyed another strong bull market through the 2000s. And both long-term peaks in the gold price – in 1980 and 2011 – were struck at unusually high gold price-to-US house price ratios. In effect, over the 53-year timeline between 1970 and 2022, this valuation metric has been quite predictive at extreme points. Extremely high gold price-to-US house price index ratios have been strongly correlated with subsequent declines in the gold price. And extremely low gold price-to-US house price index ratios have been strongly correlated with subsequent rises in the gold price.

This section of the booklet examines some potentially useful timing indicators that can assist us in determining when the odds are high that the gold price is in an uptrend (and worth the risk of buying) or when the odds are high that the gold price has entered a downtrend (where the risks of owning gold are high).

Factors that Drive Short-term Gold Demand & Supply

It's important to have a good understanding of the long-term drivers of demand for precious metals, and gold in particular, in order to gain an understanding of the stronger influences on shorter-term movements in the gold price.

Despite the view expressed previously that the gold price appears to be only fair value at best against the average US house price, short-term rallies can and do occur and the long-term trend in the gold price is always going to be upwards.

Indeed, given that global government debt has doubled since the Global Financial Crisis to over $300 trillion and rising and that most developed economies continue to run high government fiscal deficits, new highs in the gold price are very possible. And in a narrow market, like the gold market, any increase in investor demand can still lead to sharp price rallies that can be taken advantage of.

Table 3 highlights the key components of gold demand according to the World Gold Council. Traditionally, jewellery and investment are the main demand drivers, with jewellery demand fairly consistent over the medium-term. Investment demand, on the other hand, is volatile and the most significant swing factor. That said, of late, central banks' demand for gold has seen a significant increase. *Table 3* highlights that central banks' demand is up nearly three-fold from 2016 to 2022, most likely reflecting the fallout from the Russian invasion of Ukraine and the heavy sanctions imposed on Russia by the US in particular. These sanctions included a freezing of Russia US dollar reserves held abroad, a risk certain other central banks are now more alive to, and can avoid by holding their reserves in gold instead of dollar currency.

Table 3: Constituents of Annual Gold Demand

Tonnes		
	2016	2022
Investment	1,561	1,107
Jewellery	2,042	2,086
Central Banks	384	1,136
Industrial Usage	322	412
Total	**4,309**	**4,741**

Source: World Gold Council.

Gold supplies principally come from annual mining production – *circa* 3,600 tonnes annually, accounting for *circa* 70% to 75% of annual gold supply according to the World Gold Council – and the recycling of both gold jewellery and gold used for industrial purposes the remaining 25% to 30%. Central banks can also be a source of supply, but they have been net buyers for over a decade now. Most of the gold mined in history remains in existence and the 3,600-odd tonnes of newly-mined gold in 2022, along with *circa* 1,200 tonnes of recycled gold, represented an increase of just 2.3% over the existing stock of 210,000 tonnes.

Having examined a number of potential gold timing indicators, the following three indicators or strategies make most sense and appear to improve one's odds in terms of determining whether gold is in an uptrend or a downtrend:

- The Dollar Index.

- The US Long-term Real Yield.

- The Composite Coppock and 30- & 50-Week Moving Average indicators.

The Dollar Index as a Timing Indicator

While gold can be priced against any of the world's currencies, by tradition it has been traded in dollars, so that it makes sense to examine its direction against the dollar, or the Dollar Index. The Dollar Index simply tracks the performance of the dollar against a range of currencies weighted by the amount of trade done with the US.

Investment demand for gold tends to increase when the dollar is weak and *vice versa*. The question is whether the direction of the Dollar Index is a reliable indicator on which to base buy and sell decisions on gold?

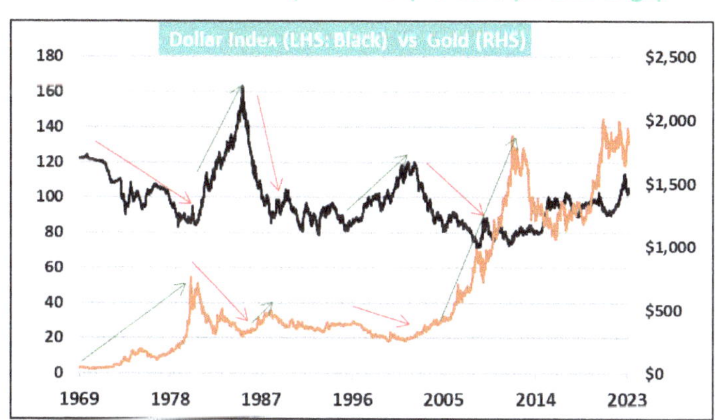

Chart 5: Dollar index (LHS: Black) *vs* Gold (RHS: Orange)

Source: World Gold Council, Bloomberg & GillenMarkets.

Chart 5 highlights a strong inverse correlation between movements in the Dollar Index and gold. In the 1970s, for example, the dollar was weak against its major trading partners. Over a similar period, gold was on the rise.

The Dollar Index was strong from 1981 to 1986, which coincided with a period of weakness for gold. However, a severe dollar correction after the 'Plaza Accord' in 1985[2] was matched by a relatively feeble rise in the gold price.

A ranging period for the dollar from the late 1980s was met by a drifting gold price. Renewed dollar strength from 1995 to 2001 led to a further leg

---

[2]   The Plaza Accord in 1985 saw several leading governments and their central banks agree collectively to intervene in currency markets to weaken the dollar.

downwards in the gold bear market that had started in January 1980. Weakness in the Dollar Index from 2001 to mid-2008 coincided with the gold bull market that also started in 2001.

The Dollar Index bottomed in late 2008, yet the gold price enjoyed a final bull market phase up until late 2011. This was unusual and, in hindsight, this last phase of the 2001 to 2011 gold bull market was probably driven by fear following the GFC. Surprisingly, strength in the Dollar Index from early 2021 to late-2022 had a more muted impact on the gold price than one might have expected. As Mark Twain once said, *"History never repeats itself but it does often rhyme"*.

It would appear that the direction of the Dollar Index has a significant influence on the gold price over short-term time horizons in the majority of occasions. With that understanding, and using weekly data, we have modelled the following to see if it provides us with a possible timing indicator for when to be in and out of gold:

- Buy gold when the gold price rises above its 30-week moving average (and when the 30-week moving average is rising) and when the Dollar Index declines below its 30-week moving average (and when its 30-week moving average is declining).

- Sell when the gold price declines below its 30-week moving average (and when the 30-week moving average is also declining) and when the Dollar Index has risen above its 30-week moving average (and when its 30-week moving average is also rising).

- When not invested in gold, place your money on deposit or buy 3-month US Treasury bills. These days, you can invest in 3-month US Treasury bills or the equivalent short-dated Eurozone government bonds using exchange-traded funds listed on stock markets.

Essentially, we are trying to buy gold when it is in a defined uptrend at the same time as the Dollar Index is in a defined downtrend and to sell out of gold when it is in a defined downtrend at the same time as the Dollar Index is in a defined uptrend.

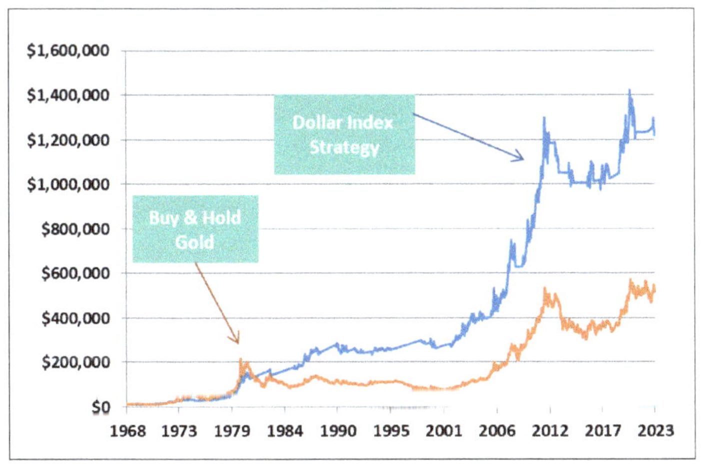

Source: GillenMarkets.

Chart 6 highlights the value of $10,000 invested on 3rd January 1968 according to the above timing indicator *versus* a 'Buy & Hold' gold strategy from that same date.

There are a couple of useful observations we can make:

- The Dollar Index / Gold timing strategy turned an investment of $10,000 on 3rd January 1968 into $1,235,851 for a 9.2% compound *per annum* return (before costs) by 24th February 2023 *versus* $522,184 for a 'Buy & Hold' strategy, or a 7.5% compound *per annum*.

- Yet, an investor was only invested in gold **55%** of the time.

- There were just 24 trades over this 55-year period from 1968 to 2023. Winning trades outpaced losing trades (15 *vs* 9).

- The largest single gain was 323% (1976 to 1981) and the worst consecutive loss was just 17% (1989 to 1992).

In conclusion, over the 1968 to 2023 period, this Dollar Index / Gold timing indicator strategy added significant value, if followed to the letter. As of 24th February 2023, this indicator is in 'Buy' mode for gold.

The US Long-term Real Yield as a Timing Indicator

A currency normally has to pay interest to a depositor (the investor), so gold has a cost compared to paper currencies as gold pays no interest. But the lower interest rates are, the less of a negative this cost comparison is for gold.

Chart 7: US 10-year Interest Rate less US CPI (1968 - 2023)

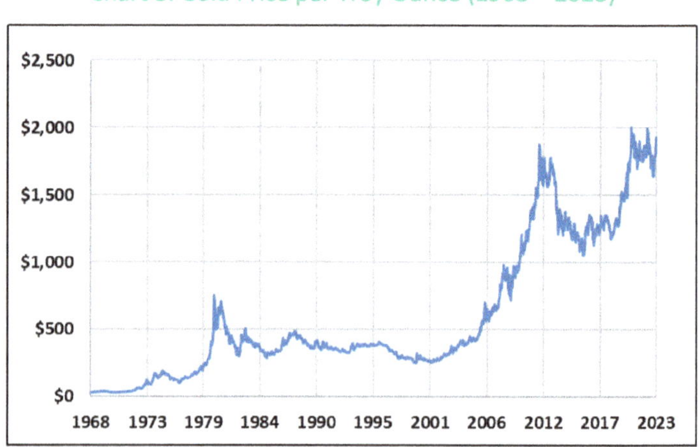

Source: GillenMarkets.

Chart 8: Gold Price per Troy Ounce (1968 – 2023)

Source: World Gold Council.

Indeed, as gold is a proven inflation hedge on a long-term basis, gold would appear to have an immediate advantage over a currency – or government bond – that offers a negative real yield (where the rate of interest on the currency or bond is below the rate of inflation).

After all, who wants to hold a currency which is not paying an interest rate above the rate of inflation? In other words, one could expect the demand for gold to rise against currencies that offer a negative real rate of interest.

Chart 7 highlights the real yield on US Government 10-year bonds since gold started to trade freely from the late 1960s. On 24th February 2023, the US 10-year bond yield was 3.94% while US consumer price inflation (CPI) was running at 6.4% annually, giving us a negative real yield of 2.46%. **Chart 7** looks encouraging, as the periods where real yields have been low to negative have coincided with gold bull markets (see **Chart 8**).

Using weekly data, we have modelled the following 'Real Yield Strategy' to see if it provides a possible timing indicator for when to be in and out of gold:

- Buy gold when the US Real yield is 2.0% or below and when the Real Yield's 30-week moving average declines below its 50-week moving average.

- Sell gold when these conditions no longer exist.

- When not invested in gold, place your money in bank deposits or buy 3-month US Treasury bills.

Essentially, we are trying to buy gold when the US 10-year Real Yield is 2% or below and when the Real Yield is in a downtrend, which is determined by when the 30-week moving average real yield declines below the 50-week moving average real yield.

Chart 9 highlights the value of $10,000 invested on 3rd January 1968 using this 'Real Yield' strategy *versus* being invested in a 'Buy & Hold' gold strategy.

There are a couple of useful observations we can make:

- An investment of $10,000 in this 'Real Yield' strategy grew to $1,643,461 for a 9.7% compound *per annum* return (before costs) by 24th February 2023 *versus* $522,184 for a 'Buy & Hold' gold strategy, or 7.5% compound *per annum*.

- Yet, an investor was only invested in gold 32% of the time. High real interest rates through the 1980s and 1990s kept an investor out of gold and in high-yielding bank deposits for nearly two decades using this strategy.

- There were just 22 trades over this 55-year period from 1968 to 2023. Winning trades considerably outpaced losing trades (18 *vs* 4).

- The largest single gain was 192% (September 1978 to November 1980) and the worst consecutive loss was just 15% (from August to December 1969).

Chart 9: Value of $10,000 Invested on 3rd January 1968

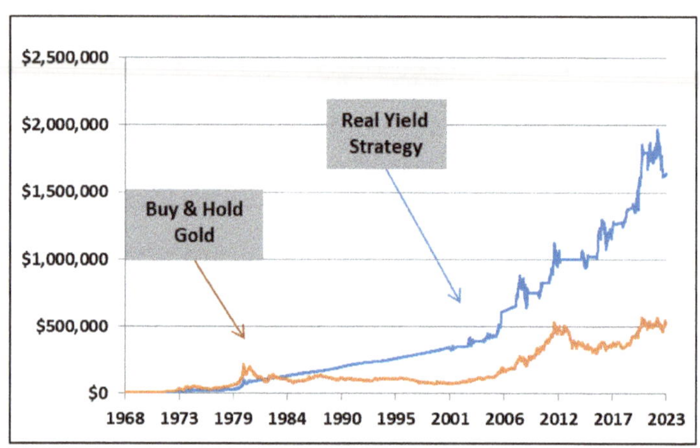

Source: GillenMarkets.

In conclusion, over the 1968 to 2023 period, the US Real Yield / Gold timing indicator also added significant value and with a considerably reduced number of losing trades. As of 24th February 2023, this indicator is in 'Sell' mode for gold reflecting the improving negative real yield.

The Composite Coppock and 30- & 50-Week Moving Average Indicator

We know from our previous work on technical indicators that the Coppock Indicator[3] has an excellent track record of generating timely 'Buy' signals after significant declines. Producing 'Buy' signals after lengthy declines also lowers risk as one can generally assume that any excessive valuation risk has been removed. As the Coppock Indicator does not provide 'Sell' signals, we sell when the 30- & 50-Week Moving Average indicator[4] gives a 'Sell' signal. The 30- & 50-Week Moving Average Indicator also provides 'Buy' signals, so that a 'Buy' signal using this strategy can be given either by the Coppock Indicator or the 30- & 50-Week Moving Average Indicator.

Using weekly data, we have modelled the following 'Coppock & Moving Average' strategy to see if it provides a possible timing indicator for when to be invested in gold and when to be out of gold:

- Buy gold when either the Coppock Indicator gives a 'Buy' signal or when the 30 & 50-Week Moving Average Indicator gives a 'Buy' signal.

- Sell gold when the 30 & 50-Week Moving Average indicator gives a 'Sell' signal.

- When not invested in gold, place your money in bank deposits or buy 3-month US Treasury bills.

The Coppock Indicator 'Buy' signal usually highlights when the demand for gold has recovered to outstrip the supply of gold in the marketplace and when the gold price is likely in a renewed uptrend. Similarly, a 'Buy' signal from the 30- & 50-Week Moving Average Indicator also tells you when the price of gold is likely back in an uptrend.

The Coppock Indicator tends to provide more timely 'Buy' signals compared to the slower-moving 30- & 50-Week Moving Average Indicator.

---

[3]   **Appendix I** explains the Coppock Indicator.
[4]   **Appendix II** explains the 30 & 50-Week Moving Average Indicator.

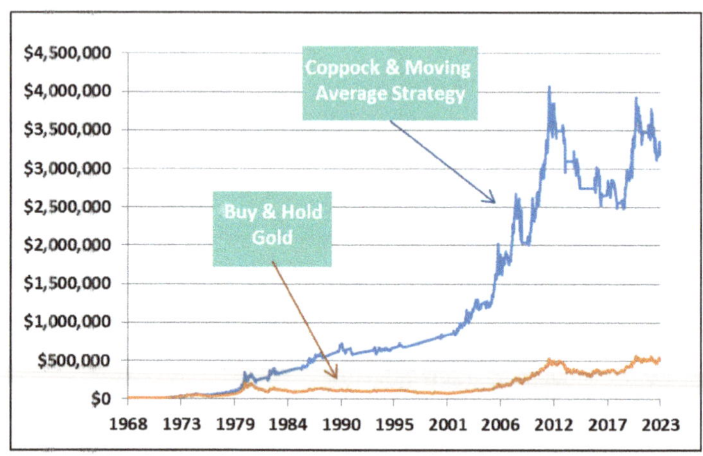

Source: GillenMarkets.

Chart 10 highlights the value of $10,000 invested on 3rd January 1968 using this 'Coppock & 30 & 50-Week Moving Average' strategy *versus* being invested in a 'Buy & Hold' gold strategy.

There are a couple of useful observations we can make:

- $10,000 invested on the 3rd January 1968 was turned into $3,192,925 for a 11.1% compound *per annum* return (before costs) to 24th February 2023 *versus* $522,184 for a 'Buy & Hold' gold investment strategy, or 7.5% compound *per annum*.

- An investor was invested in gold 66% of the time.

- There were just 21 trades over this 55-year period from 1968 to 2023. Winning trades outpaced losing trades by a narrow margin (11 *vs* 9).

- The largest single gain was 359% (1970 to 1975) and the worst consecutive loss was 27.5% (2014 to 2018).

In conclusion, over the 1968 to 2023 period, the composite 'Coppock and 30 & 50-Week Moving Average Indicator' produced the best returns, captured most of both gold bull markets (1970s and 2000s), required the least number of trades, but has had the largest consecutive loss. As of 24th February 2023, this indicator is in 'Buy' mode for gold.

In summary, all three indicators have outperformed a 'Buy & Hold' gold strategy since 1968 by healthy margins. Two of those three indicators are currently in 'Buy' mode.

There are several ways to buy and own gold:

- By purchasing physical bullion *via* a bullion dealer / broker. Here you take physical delivery of gold bars or coins.

- By purchasing certificates backed by gold bullion and guaranteed by a government.

- By buying shares or units in some collective fund structure that owns gold. Fund structures listed and traded on stock markets that exclusively own gold include investment trusts (closed-ended funds) and exchange-traded commodities (ETCs). Off-market funds can also hold gold. Funds use a global custodian to securely hold the gold bullion owned by the fund.

Exchange-traded commodities (ETCs) are open-ended securities that trade on regulated exchanges. They are secured, undated, zero-coupon guaranteed notes issued by special purpose vehicles with segregated liabilities and are generally protected by trustee structure. They are designed to accurately track the underlying performance of the individual commodity or metal.

The first gold exchange-traded commodity was introduced by State Street Global Investors, a US investment bank, with the exchange identifier or ticker code, GLD. Since 2004, however, several other ETF/ETC providers have issued gold-backed exchange-traded commodities that are also listed on stock exchanges.

Source: Bloomberg.

Chart 11 highlights both the gold price and the price of the iShares Gold ETC since its introduction in 2011. The modest difference in the two prices represents the impact of the annual management cost in the exchange-traded commodity over the period in question.

Since late 2011 annual management costs within this exchange-traded commodity of *circa* 0.25% mean that its share price has lagged the gold price by *circa* 3% at this stage (11 to 12 years later). However, buying physical bullion comes at an upfront cost – which could be up to 5% to 7% – and there is an annual storage cost if you want your physical gold stored securely.

Gold Mines Offer Leverage to the Gold Price

The gold mining industry has always been deeply cyclical, but individual gold miners have also always provided leverage to the gold price.

This is because a substantial proportion of their costs are fixed whilst their revenues increase and decrease with the market price of gold.

If, for example, a gold miner can earn a profit of, say, $550 an ounce on mined gold at a gold price of $1,836 an ounce, that same miner can probably earn a profit of $650 an ounce at a gold price of $1,936 an ounce. That's a 18% improvement in profitability for only a 5% increase in the gold price.

That said, gold exploration and mining is a capital intensive and risky business, principally due to the difficulty and unpredictability of making new gold discoveries to replenish reserves and the volatility in the gold price. And, over the years, the industry has added little long-term value.

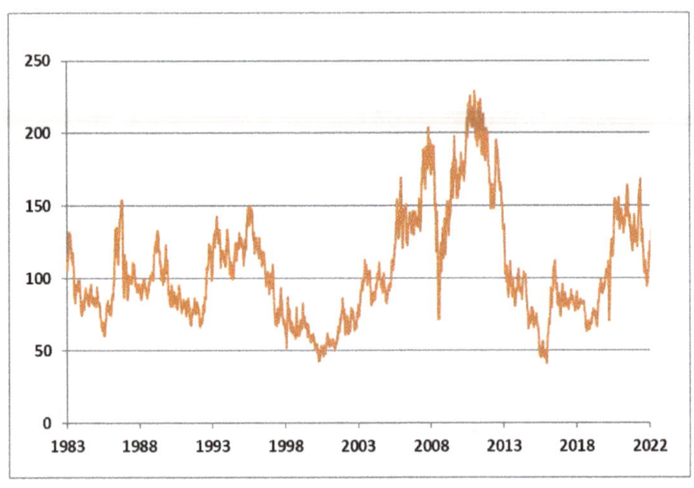

Chart 12: Philadelphia Gold & Silver Miners Index (XAU)

Source: Bloomberg.

Chart 12 highlights the Philadelphia Gold & Silver Miners Index back to the mid-1980s. Unlike standard equity indices like the FTSE All-World Index or the US S&P 500 Index, the Philadelphia Gold & Silver Miners Index has been range-bound for over 30 years. Indeed, the last gold bear market, which lasted from late-2011 to early-2016 saw this Miners Index reach the 1980s lows before starting a recovery in 2016.

Nonetheless, as with any asset class – from equities to government and corporate bonds – you can gain exposure to companies in the gold and silver mining industry by investing in individual companies, investment funds as well as exchange-traded funds that are listed and traded on stock markets. The principal European-listed exchange-traded fund for the gold miners is the

VanEck Gold Miners ETF (ticker code: GDX LN) which is listed and traded on the London Stock Exchange.

Chart 13 highlights the average gold mining industry's all-in sustaining costs of producing an ounce of gold from 2012 to 2022 inclusive, according to data provided by the World Gold Council. The dip in the cost of production from 2013 to 2016 evident in **Chart 13** reflected the impact of the gold price decline that started in September 2011. A lower selling price for gold demanded severe cost cutting across the industry in an attempt to limit the damage to profits and cash flows. More recently, higher energy costs in particular and inflation generally have led to new highs in the cost of producing an ounce of gold to $1,289 an ounce by third quarter of 2022. And the long-term trend of lower grades of gold per tonne of gold ore suggest that the line of least resistance for the cost of gold production is likely upwards.

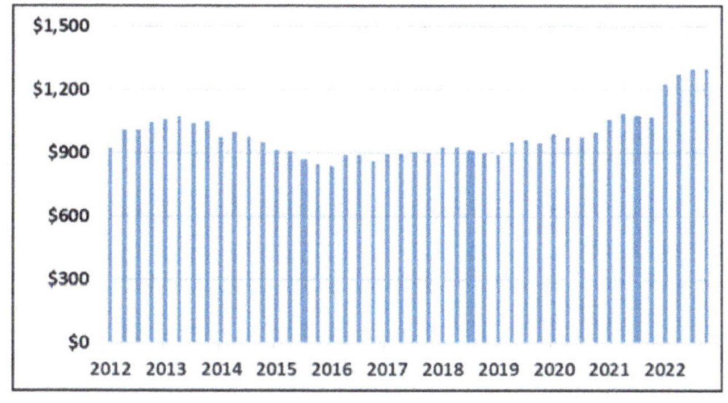

Source: World Gold Council.

Chart 14 highlights the operating margins across the gold mining industry from 2012 to 2023 inclusive. Based on the latest quarterly report on all-in sustaining costs (AISC) of the gold mining industry, the average cost of producing an ounce of gold has risen to $1,289. At the current gold price of $1,836 an ounce,[5] the gold mining industry is earning an operating margin of 30%, which is respectable but below previous margin levels. As we noted earlier, higher gold prices lead to higher operating margins without any additional capital

---

[5]   As of 24th February 2023.

investment or costs, so that the gold miners offer significant leverage to the gold price. But the margin trend in **Chart 14** also highlights the cyclicality in the industry.

Chart 14: Global Gold Mining Industry Operating Margins

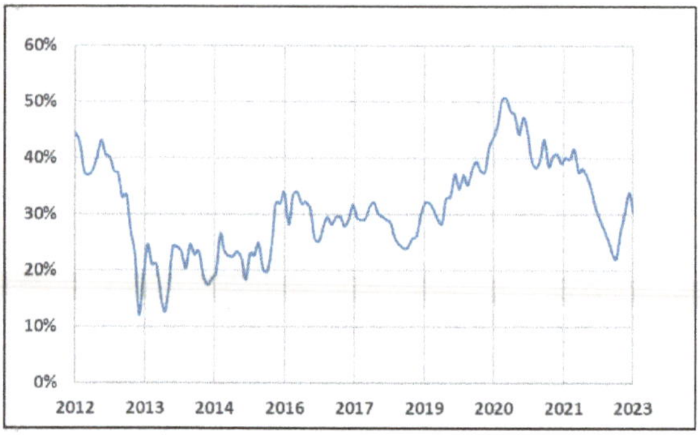

Source: World Gold Council & GillenMarkets estimates.

That said, as **Chart 12** highlights, whatever the reasons, over the decades the industry has been unable to use its profitability to compound value for shareholders. Warren Buffett probably sums it up correctly when he says: *"When a management team with a reputation for excellence meets an industry with a reputation for poor economics, it is usually the industry's reputation that remains intact".*

Equity Financiers to the Gold & Silver Mining Sector Are a Different Breed

However, companies that provide equity-like finance to precious metals miners have shown an ability to allocate capital in a productive way for shareholders. Such companies earn a return for providing equity-like finance to a miner by taking a part of the miner's output in gold and/or silver when the particular mine enters production.

In that way, their fortunes, too, are tied to the underlying precious metals prices. But they don't carry any of the operational risks associated with getting mines from exploration stage to production stage. The largest operators in this space include Franco Nevada, Wheaton Precious Metals and Royal Gold. Such companies are referred to as gold royalty and streaming companies.

While we haven't provided detailed analysis of these companies in this report, we do provide in-depth research on them *via* the members' section of the GillenMarkets website.

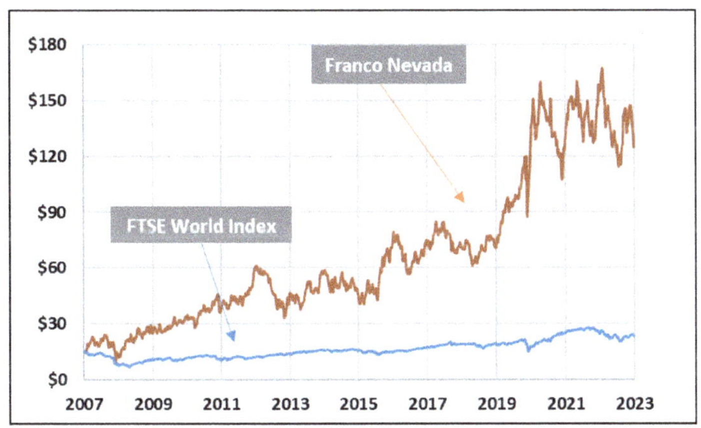

Chart 15: Franco Nevada *vs* FTSE World Index

Source: Bloomberg.

Chart 15 highlights the performance of Franco Nevada since being spun out of Newmont Mining in late-2007. Franco Nevada has not only trounced the Philadelphia Gold & Silver Miners Index, but also the FTSE World Index over this 15-year timeline.

Unlike gold (the metal), Franco Nevada pays a growing dividend to its shareholders. Since 2008, Franco Nevada has lifted its annual dividend to shareholders from $0.24 to an estimated $1.20 a share for 2022 for a current dividend yield of just over 1.0% (see **Chart 16**).

With a diversified portfolio of gold and silver reserves (owned through its royalty agreements with many different miners), Franco Nevada offers exposure to the underlying precious metals, as well as providing a growing dividend income stream.

Chart 16: Franco Nevada: Dividend per Share

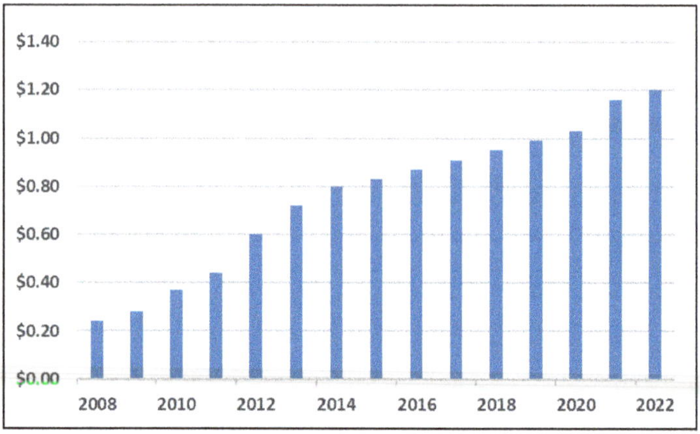

Source: Annual reports.

In a way, the precious metals royalty / streaming companies offer a middle ground between the precious metals – which represent the pure asset but generate no income – and gold miners, which traditionally have not compensated investors for the risks in their business models. It appears that the equity-like financiers are the better business model in the precious metals mining universe.

5: BITCOIN & GOLD

Cryptocurrencies have certainly caught the imagination of investors in recent years. Bitcoin was the first digital currency, and, as it remains the only truly decentralised digital currency, we will restrict our discussion in this booklet on cryptocurrencies to bitcoin.

A decentralised digital currency is one that can be traded between two parties over the Internet without any other party involved, so that there is no counter-party risk.

There's nothing particularly new in a digital currency. After all, most people are well used to paying for goods and services with credit and debit cards both of which are digital mediums of exchange. However, they are part of the banking system and using them assumes trust in the underlying banks.

The technological innovation behind the creation of bitcoin, the blockchain technology, appears to have exciting applications elsewhere, but those innovations don't lead to any income for holders of bitcoin.

Nonetheless, the concept that private citizens can by-pass the traditional banking system and trade in a currency outside the control of authorities has great attractions for bitcoin fans.

A bitcoin is a digital address identified by 27 to 34 alphanumeric characters; a string of characters stored on a computer with your digital address identifiable on a public ledger. Bitcoins are often stored on crypto exchanges.

There are no physical bitcoins, only balances kept on online public ledgers that anyone has transparent access to, that, along with bitcoin transactions, are verified and protected by a massive amount of computing power. In other words, the underlying blockchain technology facilitates instant payments or transfers of value independent of banking systems.

Is Bitcoin Money?

Trying to understand whether bitcoins are indeed a new form of money might be better approached by examining what constitutes money. Sound money should act as both a medium of exchange and a store of value, so let's examine bitcoins in that regard.

As far back as 330 BC, Aristotle, the great Greek philosopher, defined the five characteristics of sound money as:

- Durable.
- Divisible.
- Convenient.
- Consistent.
- And has use value in and of itself.

Bitcoins are probably durable. They are certainly divisible, consistent, and they are convenient, so long as you have Internet access and that others are willing to transact in bitcoins with you.

However, as a medium of exchange, transacting in bitcoins has proven to be clunky. The verification process in settling transactions is slow and expensive. In addition, the bitcoin price is volatile, so that, to date at least, bitcoins have not won the crowd over, and very few transactions in the global economy settle using bitcoins.

Bitcoin *vs* Gold

The bigger question is: are bitcoins a store of value? Similar to gold, bitcoins don't generate any income, so the inevitable question arises as to how to place a value on them.

Gold, of course, fulfils not just the first four of Aristotle's rules for sound money but also the critical fifth: it has an alternative use value. Gold has not just been used as money for 5,000 years, it has also been used as jewellery. And, in more recent times, gold has been in increasing demand for its industrial applications.

As we have seen earlier, it currently costs $1,289[6] on average to get an ounce of gold out of the ground, which we might argue should act as a base price for gold on a long-term basis. After all, if the gold price was not more than the cost of production, gold miners would sooner or later cease exploring for it and producing it. A lack of new supplies would, eventually, drive the gold price up, so long as demand remained constant.

So, gold's intrinsic value is derived from its use as jewellery and in industrial applications, even if it was never again used as money.

And I consider this an important *caveat*. Over the years gold's use as money has often wavered. As a recent example, from 1980 to 2001, investors and central banks no longer bought gold for its 'store of value'. And the gold price spent those 21 years in the doldrums losing *circa* 70% of its value while most other assets gained in value over that same period. But at least an investor in gold knew that there was a base value for gold, its intrinsic value or the cost of production for its use as jewellery and in industry.

Bitcoin fans have to be able to answer the same question; if bitcoins produce no income, what gives them value? Some argue that bitcoins' 'alternative use value' is in war-torn countries where citizens can leave such regions and recover their savings and wealth *via* the Internet elsewhere. It's not an unreasonable point. And, like a piece of art, the value is in the eye of the beholder. So long as someone is willing to buy bitcoins at a certain price and there's a willing seller then you have a market.

As with gold, however, the critical issue underpinning intrinsic value is a lack of new supplies. Annual mining production adds under 2.0% to existing gold mining reserve ounces. This lack of supply is what has allowed the gold price to keep pace with inflation and, thus, act as a store of value of the millennia.

Bitcoin fans argue that the supply of bitcoins is limited to 21 million, so that they will always retain a scarcity factor, and one that is better even than gold.

It's a neat argument. For this writer, however, I have yet to be convinced about why a new decentralised cryptocurrency cannot be brought forward on the same or alternative basis as bitcoin has. Bitcoin has been created electronically and I have trouble understanding what is unique about that. In

---

gold's case, it has a 5,000-year old track record of limited supplies and durability.

Gold has been a better store of value than most paper currencies throughout history. Yet, as the supply of gold cannot always be increased at the same pace as global trade expands, there has never been enough gold around to facilitate the settlement of faster expanding global trade. Gold is an excellent store of value, but it has never been an ideal medium of exchange.

And gold's limitations over the years to act as a functioning medium of exchange is the core reason for the development and acceptance of paper currencies, and governments' support for them starting in the late 18th century.

Bitcoin *vs* Paper Currencies

People have traded with each other in goods and services since time began. Paper money and credit facilitate trade, and to be accepted as payment each must be trusted and have intrinsic value. We receive payment for our goods and services, and we lodge our payment into the banking system. We trust the banks to safeguard our money.

Intrinsic value for paper currencies comes from their ability to pay interest and, thus, to provide a return to investors that compensates them for inflation and the risk of loss should the bank fail. So, bank deposits, or paper currencies, should offer a return over and above inflation on a medium- to long-term basis.

The risk-averse saver in society, that person who saves his/her money in bank deposits, is entitled to earn an income that is above inflation as compensation for the risks involved. People saving in bank deposits will only do so over the long-term if they are rewarded for the risks that inflation rates outpace deposit interest rates or that reckless bank lending imperils their capital (that risk crystallised in 2008).

But what backs paper currencies and underpins their intrinsic value? Governments, of course! A sound banking system and a country's currency is underpinned by a government's ability to raise revenue through taxes, not just today, but into the indefinite future. Paper money in a trusted banking system is both a medium of exchange and a potential store of value.

However, as paper money can be created at will by both banks and governments (*via* central banks), not all paper currencies have acted as a store of value. Think of the German Reichsmark after WW1 and, more recently, the Argentinian peso, the Zimbabwean dollar, the Venezuelan bolívar, the Turkish lira, the Syrian pound and quite possibly the Russian ruble – all worthless as a store of value after their respective governments spent recklessly and printed money in huge quantities to try and pay for that spending.

Summary

Bitcoins are potentially a new medium of exchange outside the traditional banking system but appear to have failed at that task to date. And, given that someone has invented them out of thin air, this writer remains unconvinced that bitcoins will be in limited supply for long. Indeed, if replication is possible, the new supply would likely be unlimited, in which case the price of bitcoin would head to zero. Hence, it's a leap too far for me to consider them a store of value. Time may prove me wrong, but I'm happy to avoid this new financial innovation!

Appendix I: UNDERSTANDING & CALCULATING THE COPPOCK INDICATOR

The Coppock Indicator was devised by Edwin Coppock in the US in the 1950s, who was asked by his church, for whom he was an adviser, to identify a good time to buy into the markets for long-term investing after a serious decline. He countered by asking the church how long it took, on average, for people to get over a bereavement. The church felt it took on average 11 to 14 months. Coppock knew that the impact of bear (down) markets on an investor was psychologically similar to bereavement. So, if it took 11 to 14 months on average to recover from bereavement, Coppock figured that he should not expect recovery in markets after a recession-led decline until the same time had passed.

He set about developing a technical indicator to help him better gauge when markets had turned. The Coppock Indicator, as it is now known, is a monthly indicator and represents the sum of a 14-month rate of change and an 11-month rate of change, with the combined rate of change then averaged out over a 10-month period, and with a higher weight attached to the most recent month and progressively less weight to the other nine months. It sounds complex but it is relatively straightforward to measure using a spreadsheet, and we include such a spreadsheet in the members' area of our website, and update it on a monthly basis.

The Coppock Indicator gives 'Buy' signals but it is not designed to provide 'Sell' signals. Nonetheless, as a 'Buy' indicator, it has an excellent long-term track record on the major equity markets and a decent track record with gold.

As **Chart 17** highlights, a 'Buy' signal is given when the indicator drops below zero and then turns upwards from a negative position (the blue arrows highlight a number of 'Buy' signals from 1969 to 2023) . However, like any technical indicator, the Coppock Indicator does not work all the time.

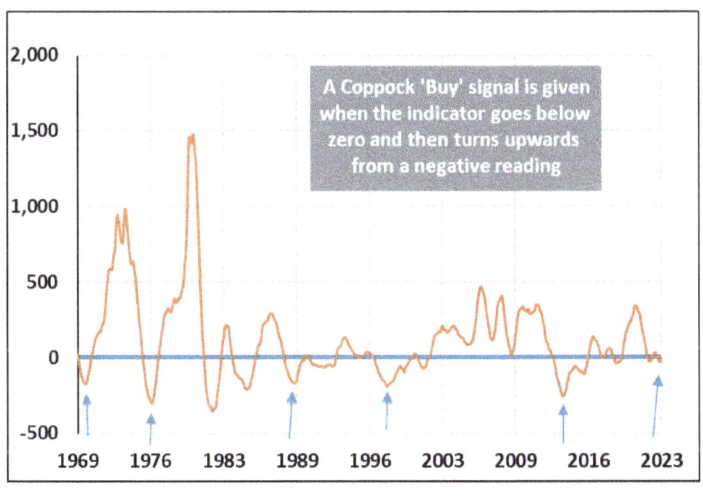

Source: GillenMarkets.

Coppock Indicator Calculations

For the index of your choice, the following guidelines should allow you to create your own Coppock Indicator. The next page has the actual calculations for the Euro Stoxx 50 Index leading up to the 'Buy' signal at the end of January 2023.

1. In Columns 1 & 2, note the end of month date and value for the previous 14 months.
2. In Column 3, note the index value for 14 months ago. In Column 4, express that difference as a percentage.
3. In Column 5, note the index value for 11 months ago. In Column 6, express that difference as a percentage.
4. In Column 7, add the 14- and 11-month percentage differences.
5. In Column 8, multiply Column 7 by 10.
6. In Column 9, drop down a month and multiply Column 7 by 9.
7. In Column 10, drop down a month and multiply Column 7 by 8.
8. And so on – in each successive Column, drop down a month and multiply by one less until you come to Column 18.
9. In Column 18, sum Columns 8 to 17.

10. In Column 19, divide Column 18 by 10.

11. After point 10, you have a weighted average of the end of month data stretching back 24 months.

12. Only readings that have a value for each of the Columns 8 to 17 are included in the series.

13. Now plot the series on a chart (optional).

14. The indicator provides a buy signal when it dips below zero and then gives a less negative reading.

Gold - Coppock Spreadsheet Example

1	2	3	4	5	6	7	8	9	10	11	12	13	14	15	16	17	18	19
		14m	%Δ	11m	%Δ	Add 2+4	Col7 X10	Col7 -1mx9	Col7 -2mx9	Col7 -3mx9	Col7 -4mx9	Col7 -5mx9	Col7 -6m x9	Col7 -7m x9	Col7 -8m x9	Col7 -9m x9	Sum Col8 -Col10	Divide Col18 by 10
31/07/2019	3,466.9																	
31/08/2019	3,426.8																	
30/09/2019	3,569.5																	
31/10/2019	3,604.4																	
30/11/2019	3,703.6																	
31/12/2019	3,745.2																	
31/01/2020	3,640.9																	
29/02/2020	3,329.5																	
31/03/2020	2,786.9																	
30/04/2020	2,927.9																	
31/05/2020	3,050.2																	
30/06/2020	3,234.0																	
31/07/2020	3,174.3																	
31/08/2020	3,272.5																	
30/09/2020	3,193.6	3,466.9	-7.9	3604.4	-11.4	-19.3	-192.8											
31/10/2020	2,958.0	3,426.8	-13.7	3703.6	-20.1	-33.8	-338.1	-173.5										
30/11/2020	3,492.5	3,569.5	-2.2	3745.2	-6.7	-8.9	-89.0	-304.3	-154.2									
31/12/2020	3,553.0	3,604.4	-1.4	3640.9	-2.4	-3.8	-38.4	-80.1	-270.5	-135.0								
31/01/2021	3,481.4	3,703.6	-6.0	3329.5	4.6	-1.4	-14.4	-34.6	-71.2	-236.7	-115.7							
28/02/2021	3,636.4	3,745.2	-2.9	2786.9	30.5	27.6	275.8	-12.9	-30.7	-62.3	-202.9	-96.4						
31/03/2021	3,919.2	3,640.9	7.6	2927.9	33.9	41.5	415.0	248.2	-11.5	-26.9	-53.4	-169.1	-77.1					

1	2	3	4	5	6	7	8	9	10	11	12	13	14	15	16	17	18	19
		14m	%Δ	11m	%Δ	Add 2+4	Col7 X10	Col7 -1mx9	Col7 -2mx9	Col7 -3mx9	Col7 -4mx9	Col7 -5mx9	Col7 -6m x9	Col7 -7m x9	Col7 -8m x9	Col7 -9m x9	Sum Col8 -Col10	Divide Col18 by 10
30/04/2021	3,974.7	3,329.5	19.4	3050.2	30.3	49.7	496.9	373.5	220.6	-10.1	-23.0	-44.5	-135.2	-57.8				
31/05/2021	4,039.5	2,786.9	44.9	3234.0	24.9	69.9	698.5	447.2	332.0	193.1	-8.6	-19.2	-35.6	-101.4	-38.6			
30/06/2021	4,064.3	2,927.9	38.8	3174.3	28.0	66.9	668.5	628.7	397.5	290.5	165.5	-7.2	-15.4	-26.7	-67.6	-19.3	2014.5	201.5
31/07/2021	4,089.3	3,050.2	34.1	3272.5	25.0	59.0	590.3	601.7	558.8	347.8	249.0	137.9	-5.7	-11.5	-17.8	-33.8	2416.6	241.7
31/08/2021	4,196.4	3,234.0	29.8	3193.6	31.4	61.2	611.6	531.2	534.8	489.0	298.1	207.5	110.3	-4.3	-7.7	-8.9	2761.7	276.2
30/09/2021	4,048.1	3,174.3	27.5	2958.0	36.9	64.4	643.8	550.4	472.2	468.0	419.1	248.5	166.0	82.7	-2.9	-3.8	3044.0	304.4
31/10/2021	4,250.6	3,272.5	29.9	3492.5	21.7	51.6	515.9	579.4	489.3	413.2	401.1	349.3	198.8	124.5	55.2	-1.4	3125.1	312.5
30/11/2021	4,063.1	3,193.6	27.2	3553.0	14.4	41.6	415.8	464.3	515.0	428.1	354.2	334.3	279.4	149.1	83.0	27.6	3050.7	305.1
31/12/2021	4,298.4	2,958.0	45.3	3481.4	23.5	68.8	687.8	374.2	412.7	450.7	367.0	295.1	267.4	209.6	99.4	41.5	3205.4	320.5
31/01/2022	4,174.6	3,492.5	19.5	3636.4	14.8	34.3	343.3	619.0	332.6	361.1	386.3	305.8	236.1	200.6	139.7	49.7	2974.2	297.4
28/02/2022	3,924.2	3,553.0	10.4	3919.2	0.1	10.6	105.8	309.0	550.3	291.1	309.5	321.9	244.6	177.1	133.7	69.9	2512.8	251.3
31/03/2022	3,902.5	3,481.4	12.1	3974.7	-1.8	10.3	102.8	95.2	274.6	481.5	249.5	258.0	257.5	183.5	118.1	66.9	2087.4	208.7
30/04/2022	3,802.9	3,636.4	4.6	4039.5	-5.9	-1.3	-12.8	92.5	84.6	240.3	412.7	207.9	206.4	193.1	122.3	59.0	1606.1	160.6
31/05/2022	3,789.2	3,919.2	-3.3	4064.3	-6.8	-10.1	-100.9	-11.5	82.2	74.0	206.0	343.9	166.3	154.8	128.8	61.2	1104.8	110.5
30/06/2022	3,454.9	3,974.7	-13.1	4089.3	-15.5	-28.6	-285.9	-90.8	-10.2	72.0	63.5	171.6	275.1	124.7	103.2	64.4	487.5	48.8
31/07/2022	3,708.1	4,039.5	-8.2	4196.4	-11.6	-19.8	-198.4	-257.3	-80.7	-9.0	61.7	52.9	137.3	206.3	83.2	51.6	47.6	4.8
31/08/2022	3,517.3	4,064.3	-13.5	4048.1	-13.1	-26.6	-265.7	-178.6	-228.8	-70.6	-7.7	51.4	42.3	103.0	137.6	41.6	-375.5	-37.5
30/09/2022	3,318.2	4,089.3	-18.9	4250.6	-21.9	-40.8	-407.9	-239.2	-158.7	-200.2	-60.5	-6.4	41.1	31.7	68.7	68.8	-862.6	-86.3
31/10/2022	3,617.5	4,196.4	-13.8	4063.1	-11.0	-24.8	-247.6	-367.1	-212.6	-138.9	-171.6	-50.4	-5.1	30.8	21.2	34.3	-1107.0	-110.7
30/11/2022	3,964.7	4,048.1	-2.1	4298.4	-7.8	-9.8	-98.2	-222.8	-326.3	-186.0	-119.0	-143.0	-40.3	-3.8	20.6	10.6	-1108.5	-110.8
31/12/2022	3,793.6	4,250.6	-10.8	4174.6	-9.1	-19.9	-198.8	-88.4	-198.1	-285.5	-159.4	-99.2	-114.4	-30.3	-2.6	10.3	-1166.3	-116.6
31/01/2023	[illegible]	[illegible]	[illegible]	[illegible]	[illegible]	[illegible]	[illegible]	[illegible]	[illegible]	[illegible]	[illegible]	[illegible]	[illegible]	[illegible]	[illegible]	[illegible]	-909.3	-90.4

Note: The Coppock Indicator is outlined in more detail in our booklet *Timing the Markets* and can be followed in the members' area of our website and/or bought online by non-members at **www.gillenmarkets.com**.

Appendix II: UNDERSTANDING & CALCULATING THE 30- & 50-WEEK MOVING AVERAGE INDICATOR

Next up is the 30 & 50-Week Moving Average Indicator as a market 'Buy' and 'Sell' signal. As an indicator, it tends to be slower to react to turns in markets, but still very useful in highlighting trending markets (markets that are in either a defined uptrend or defined downtrend). Similar to the Coppock Indicator, the 30 & 50-Week Moving Average Indicator is mechanical in nature, with no subjectivity or input required by the user (apart from using a spreadsheet).

The 30 & 50-week moving averages for the gold price are calculated by obtaining the average gold price over the last 30 weeks and last 50 weeks. Like any moving average, the 30-week and 50-week moving averages help iron out the short-term volatility apparent in the underlying market and can assist investors to more easily identify the underlying trend.

The defining characteristic of this indicator is that a 'Buy' signal on gold is generated only when the 30-week moving average line crosses upwards through the 50-week moving average line. Similarly, a 'Sell' signal is given only when the 30-week moving average line crosses down through the 50-week moving average line.

It is a slower-moving indicator than, say, the Coppock Indicator, but it can be used on any market and gives both 'Buy' and 'Sell' signals. Although the main benefit of the indicator, in our view, is that it can keep an investor out of deep bear markets, it is a slow-moving indicator and, thus, tends to get an investor out of the market later into a downturn and back into the market later in a recovery. In other words, it's a lagging indicator. One must also recognise that this indicator has limited value in ranging markets (markets that are trading sideways with no defined uptrend or downtrend).

Source. GillenMarkets.

30- & 50-Week Moving Average Calculations

Date	Gold Price	30-Week Moving Average	50-Week Moving Average
05-Nov-21	1,816.80		
12-Nov-21	1,868.50		
19-Nov-21	1,851.60		
26-Nov-21	1,785.50		
03-Dec-21	1,782.00		
10-Dec-21	1,782.90		
17-Dec-21	1,803.80		
24-Dec-21	1,811.20		
31-Dec-21	1,828.60		
07-Jan-22	1,797.40		
14-Jan-22	1,816.50		
21-Jan-22	1,831.80		
28-Jan-22	1,784.90		
04-Feb-22	1,806.60		

Date	Gold Price	30-Week Moving Average	50-Week Moving Average
11-Feb-22	1,840.80		
18-Feb-22	1,898.60		
25-Feb-22	1,887.60		
04-Mar-22	1,966.60		
11-Mar-22	1,985.00		
18-Mar-22	1.929.30		
25-Mar-22	1,954.20		
01-Apr-22	1,919.10		
08-Apr-22	1,941.60		
15-Apr-22	1,970.90		
22-Apr-22	1,931.00		
29-Apr-22	1,911.70		
06-May-22	1,882.80		
13-May-22	1,808.20		
20-May-22	1,842.10		
27-May-22	1,851,30	1,862.96	
03-Jun-22	1,845.40	1,863.92	
10-Jun-22	1,871.50	1,864.02	
17-Jun-22	1,835.60	1,863.48	
24-Jun-22	1,826.50	1,864.85	
01-Jul-22	1,801.50	1,865.50	
08-Jul-22	1,742.30	1,864.15	
15-Jul-22	1,703.60	1,860.81	
22-Jul-22	1,727.40	1,858.01	
29-Jul-22	1,762.90	1,855.02	
5-Aug-22	1,772.60	1,855.00	
12-Aug-22	1,798.60	1,854.40	
19-Aug-22	1,747.60	1,851.59	
26-Aug-22	1,736.10	1,849.97	
02-Sep-22	1,713.00	1,846.85	
09-Sep-22	1,718.80	1,842.78	
16-Sep-22	1,672.80	1,835.25	

Date	Gold Price	30-Week Moving Average	50-Week Moving Average
23-Sep-22	1,645.30	1,827.18	
30-Sep-22	1,662.40	1,817.04	
07-Oct-22	1,700.50	1,807.55	
14-Oct-22	1,641.70	1,797.97	
21-Oct-22	1,651.00	1,787.86	1,812.98
28-Oct-22	1,644.80	1,778.72	1,808.51
04-Nov-22	1,676.60	1,769.88	1,805.01
11-Nov-22	1,769.40	1,763.17	1,804.69
18-Nov-22	1,754.40	1,757.28	1,804.14
25-Nov-22	1,754.00	1,752.02	1,803.56
02-Dec-22	1,795.90	1,749.13	1,803.40
09-Dec-22	1,793.00	1,748.62	1,803.04
16-Dec-22	1,790.00	1,746.88	1,802.21
23-Dec-22	1,801.20	1,745.21	1,802.34
30-Dec-22	1,826.20	1,744.51	1,802.53

Average of the 50 weeks from 5th Nov 2021 to 14th Oct 2022

Note: The 30 & 50-Week Moving Average Indicator is outlined in more detail in our booklet *Timing the Markets* and can be followed in the members' area of our website and/or bought online by non-members at **www.gillenmarkets.com**.

Intelligent Gold Investing

Gold is money, and its durability, density, consistency and limited new supplies have resulted in it being the only currency to have acted as a true store of value over the millennia.

This booklet was written by Rory Gillen, founder of GillenMarkets and author of *3 Steps to Investment Success*, published in 2012. It outlines the physical characteristics of gold that underpin its use as jewellery and, more recently, in complex industrial applications. As gold yields no income, it cannot be valued in a conventional sense, so the booklet offers guidance on how to judge gold's intrinsic value and how one can value gold relative to other hard assets such as US house prices.

The booklet also introduces you to three separate and highly useful technical indicators that provide a risk-controlled way of determining when gold is worth buying. All three indicators have outperformed a 'Buy & Hold' gold strategy since 1968 by wide margins.

Finally, there's a discussion on the merits or otherwise of bitcoin, which some argue is the new digital gold.

Gillen.

E: info@gillenmarkets.com
T: +353 1 2871400
W: www.gillenmarkets.com